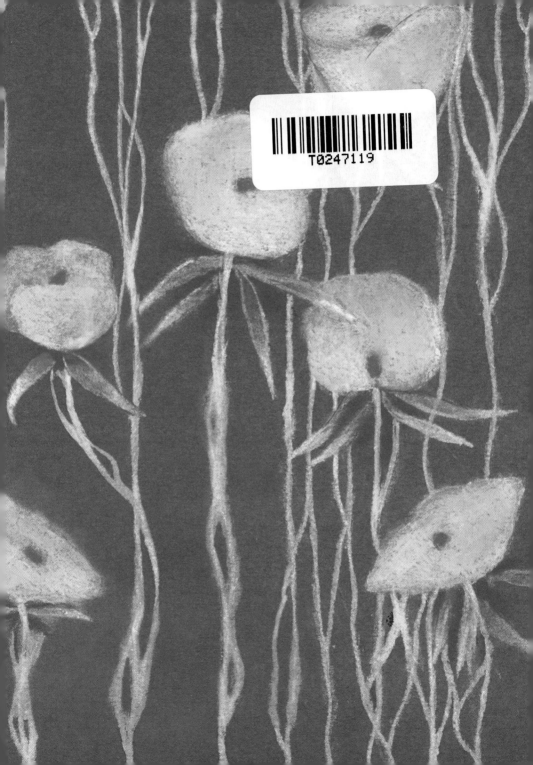

T0247119

a full circle

a full circle

Namrita
Bachchan

HARPER DESIGN
An Imprint of HarperCollins Publishers

First published in India by HarperDesign 2022
An imprint of HarperCollins *Publishers*
Building No 10, Tower A, 4th Floor, DLF Cyber City, Phase II,
Gurugram – 122002
www.harpercollins.co.in

2 4 6 8 10 9 7 5 3 1
Text and art copyright © Namrita Bachchan 2022

P-ISBN: 978-93-5489-471-8
E-ISBN: 978-93-5489-472-5

Namrita Bachchan asserts the moral right
to be identified as the author of this work.

Cover design: Bonita Vaz-Shimray

Printed and bound at Thomson Press (India) Ltd

🅕🅘🅞🅨 HarperCollinsIn

made with love
for Noah,
and You

poetry is a wheel in my heart

the more
i read,

the MORE
i delight

the more
i delight,
the deeper
i feel

the deeper
i feel,
the sweeter
i breathe

the sweeter
i breathe,
the less
i despair

the less
    i despair,
the bolder
        i grow

the bolder
i grow,
the closer
i look

the closer
i Look,
the further
i see

the further
i see,
the more
i believe

the more
i believe,
the kinder
i speak

the kinder
i speak,
the keener
i hear

the keener
i hear,
the less
i compare

the less
i compare,

the sounder
i sleep

the sounder
i sleep,
the FULLER
i dream

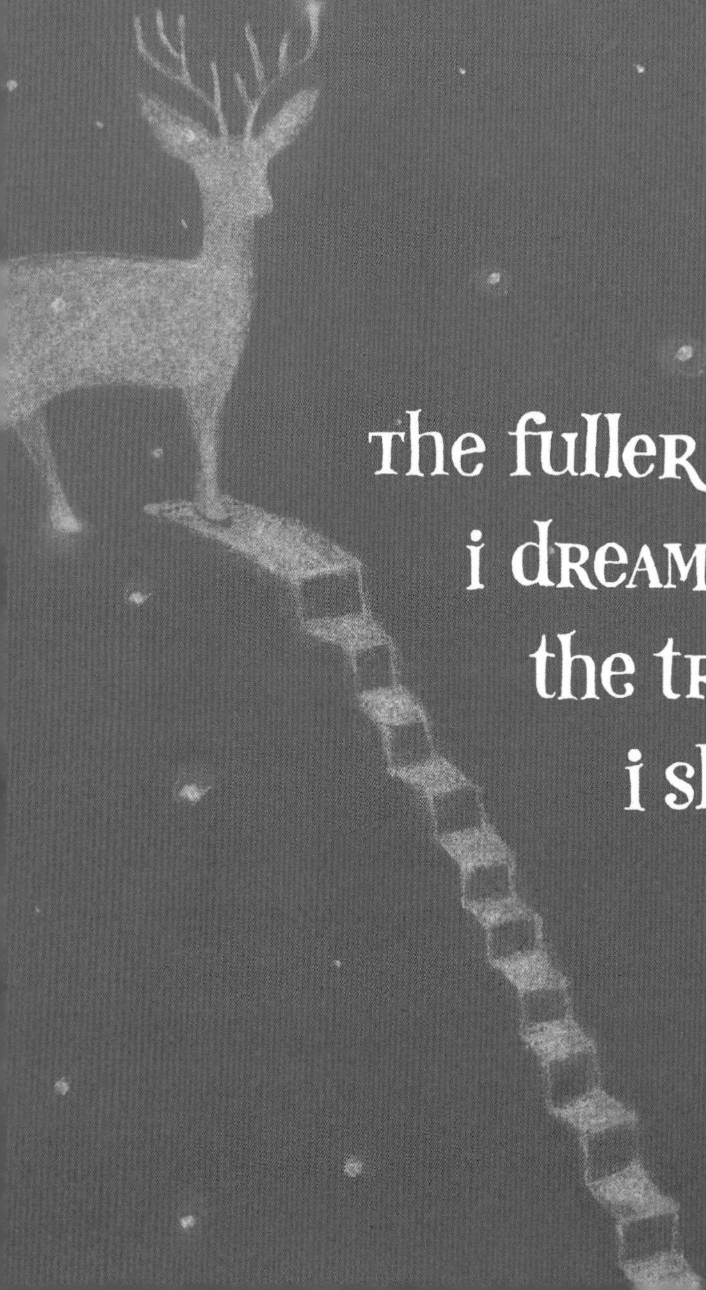

the fuller
i dream,
the truer
i shine

the truer
i shine,
the lighter
i feel

the lighter
i feel,
the freer
my mind

the freer
my mind,
the more
i read

the more
i read,
the more
i delight...

SHE knows this book is for her, and made me promise that I would draw her with a friend in each image of her adventure. It is a promise I have kept. *A Full Circle*, therefore, is a true collaboration between us—mother and child.

I had attempted to make a children's book once before. The experience of parenthood, however, so deeply shifted my perspective that it wasn't until I was in the daily presence of a curious and vibrant innocence that I could genuinely begin to navigate their mystifying world—a world to which I had once belonged myself.

I wrote this poem one evening when Noah was around two years old. In fact, I didn't so much write it as come into it, because the words themselves began to cascade spontaneously in my mind, growing organically in both directions to form verse. All of a sudden, I had something meaningful I could preserve for her, something hymnal for her to carry through the course of her own life as a kind of heirloom, connecting her inner voice to mine. So began the creative process.

The sentiment at the heart of this poem is one that, as a visual artist, I have contemplated often—*the closer I look, the further I see*—especially whilst engaged in the act of photography, given my eye is instinctively drawn to the small and commonplace over the looming and manifest. Or rather, as is my belief, the small and commonplace which often reveals itself to be the looming and manifest.

The photographs I've made of Noah since her birth, which are the vision behind this picture-book, are on one level a pictorial documentation of her personal evolution, and on another, a broader, more objective response to observing childhood in motion—that evanescent yet limitless period of a human being's time on earth, when they are still wont to be led by forces of magic. To my understanding, the closest parallel is the experience of poetry, which seems to contain a circumspect sense of wonder whilst conveying essential truths. Poetry not just in its literal form, but the poetics of all phenomena: sound, colour, atmosphere, expression, emotion, texture, quality of light, depth of shadow, solitude, numbers, pattern, melody, narrative, love, memory, touch... In essence, I endeavoured to guide Noah towards learning how to read the world in a lyrical and prescient way, for her own enrichment, and to remember to do so thereafter.

The more I read, the more I delight. Language, and the mysterious joys of the imagination have played a vital role in my own existence, shaping so many of my choices. In a sense, this book acknowledges all those voices that have travelled down to me through reading, all those voices that have contoured and coloured my own.

The cyclical nature of the poem, itself a metaphor for all life, gives the lines a cadence making them easy to memorize, and calls to mind that evocative medieval term *carmen matricale*, meaning primitive or maternal song, which takes its root in the Latin word matrix, meaning womb. It is both sweet and surprising that over the past year of picturizing *A Full Circle*, I found myself repeating the lines internally in the manner of a personal incantation. It is my hope that Noah, and perhaps even you, will find comfort and courage should you do the same.

So there it is, a little insight into how this work came to be, and the spirited child who inspired it. What remains is to express a few words of gratitude, as I could not have made this passage on my own. Every book needs help on its journey from the mind to the shelf; this one owes its wings to Bonita Vaz-Shimray, Ketanbhai Mehta, Chiki Sarkar, my family, and above all Neville Tuli.